D1554699

DUST
BOWL
VENUS

DUST BOWL
Venus

POEMS

STELLA BERATLIS

Sixteen Rivers Press

Copyright © 2021 by Stella Beratlis
All rights reserved
Printed in the United States of America

Special thanks to David Sibbet
for his support of Sixteen Rivers Press

Published by Sixteen Rivers Press
P.O. Box 640663
San Francisco, CA 94164-0663

ISBN: 978-1-939639-25-7
LCCN: 2020-944927

Cover art: *Valley Evening with Caterpillar,* Jim Damron, oil on panel
Design: Frank M. Young

for Demetra Vasiliki Paras, with all my love,
and
Hazel Marie Houser-Spencer
(1922–96)
In memoriam

CONTENTS

Regret Bench

Spacetime Curvature

Scratch under the hardpan
    turn over a shovelful of soil,
    inhale. Obscured data lies in wait;

you will discover it. For years,
pay undue attention to the things this place is not:

the negative capability of valley,
    the not-reaching after facts.

    And then.
    And then.

And then the Hotel Hughson is demolished.
    We stand in the middle of J Street
        watch masonry tumble in on itself
        hot planet's crushing pressure
        a mushroom of dust plumes first into the sky
            then freezes, snapshotting memory.

    Remember where we are?
We live on a seasonal lake bed. We live in lowland regions on Dust
    Bowl Venus.

In this valley, our forefathers are deserters:
    landholders, railroad men,
    Comstock plunderers.

Their secrets deposited inside the city's darkest heart.
A drainage, a tule berm, a vernal pool.

Shelter Belt

I'm on my way
Gonna wade right in
I'm going down to the river of Jordan
And let the cool waters cleanse my soul

—Hazel Houser, "The River of Jordan"

What Grows Here

1. *You Remember the Names*

You might say we get emotional, when, along 99 South,
we see trucks and trailers pulling those bales, those bales
suitable for consumption, precise rectangles fresh
with swagger and sway, precarious promise
of bit and endless chew, that livestock
fodder. Then trailer of tomatoes, in and out
for pre-processing baths while
factory gates remain open
all August long.
    Inside, the head mechanic is a poet,
tunes words and engines, writes lines
on the line. His kind is an heirloom,
a Boxcar Willie or Purple Cherokee
that ripens too late for the cannery
but is perfect for the yard. And oh,
we toil for it outside,
our giant Oxhearts
in cages.

2. *Myrtle of the Tomatoes*

We see you
in the garden,
no Massey Ferguson,

no almond dust.
You grow enough for all,
you sing to no choir.

O Myrtle,
you transform
even the back alley
into rows and furrows,
furrows and rows.

3. Holy Basil

At the intersection of Texas and Crows Landing
he stands, rosemary in pocket, the man who grows the basil.
All of his life packed—the work of it, the sore knees, the sweat—
into orderly cylinders of regret, fresh with summer's
bursting heart. He muses on the city's blurred stars:
    the songwriter who—
        the baby who—
           the Marine who—
              the baker, who carried a fresh sourdough right to your
              door, the geometry of her face doubled by her straight
                  hair—
All of those sacred, incomparable ones,
those who live, die, and live again,
they are here;
they are making mud
out of dry soil.

Perfect Love Song

We wake,
Paganini-stung
on Steiner. Paganini-
plucked, where the bow
scrapes out stories
an ardent heart
might believe,
bone-and-ligament
narratives. Rimbaud
in Paris, wine
and Blue '59, sports car
night ride across
a twinkle-lit city,
and Hells Bells
Concerto No.1
still playing
on the turntable.
In the warped space
of time travelers,
I'll take the pop slide
pop slide of needle,
riding the label for hours
after the music
already ended . . .

Ergo Paganini, ergo you
          whom I love always
inside the oddball
random letters,
the run-out groove—
Roots, knots, and wind—

I see your structure.
Words you reused
in letters back to me,
the bow's slicing arc,
the many Januaries
of my demise, et cetera.
Except it's your end—
coming just after drunken
words, *All the boys*
been sayin' it: you look good.
But Paul, I'm dreaming
of perfect fifths, sickness,
and pizzicato. You are sprung
and strung with gut.
You are stretched,
dried, and twisted
Pacific. You burrow into
my skin like ticks;
I am held inside
your morning.

In Other News

I started the dough two days ago
I used time as an ingredient
from a cookbook for beginners

where we are instructed
to respect baking time
time as an ingredient time

as the flavor-unlocking key time
as a vital factor for success
not the same ingredient required

to construct the bones of new stanzas
not from leftover yeast and flour
of last winter I mixed it in

and left some big goddamn clumps
and now you taste pockets of salt
and overwhelming mouthfeel

dense crumb an uncooked lump of this
along with ground coffee beans
and filtered water all of my secret apocalypse

ingredients developed by my precisely calibrated
family this uncle who died last week
his brain's own unit of time

not recognized by the International System of Units
although really it should
since we all watch our loved ones die

like that or myriad other ways
see and know them from a distance
how close to this galaxy's main star

his desiccated heart traveled
I mean the unit of time required
the speed of light I think

that is what they mean

Inventory of Household Items

(I'm conducting a survey for insurance purposes.)

Clipboard, please note:
      my Lucky Strike sign,
its every atom of neon trembling
      to light in noir silhouette
the wasted extravagance
      of set jaw, knife block of face.

Next, a cigar box on the coffee table
      contains one 64-page
         spiral-bound manuscript book,
      six staves per page,
and a No. 1
Ticonderoga pencil.

Consider the stave,
      the five parallel lines
         and spaces between them;
      sixty-four times six,
         a multiplicity of staves,
            a murder of telephone wires
singing the dots, withholding the words.

(In the event of fire or disaster, I will need this list.)

Listen only: Those dots are one-minded, fly off together
      as one constellation,
         are written—in the softest
of pencils—gentle, black-filled dots,

easily wiped off as needed,
      easily repeated.
The smoke of this dream stays in the air
      long after the trombone-like vocal phrasing
has been erased, long after that night
      when all the stars fell.
Those little houses are gone.

Clipboards hold only temporary data,
      so where does this document get filed?
Maybe next to the postcard on the fridge,
      an ode to domesticity,
chained to the imaginary mundane
      in Louis Armstrong's blue kitchen—
            I allowed the dreams to make a spiral steeple,
      the same way Watts Towers was built:
took your broken plates, a chipped tile from the patio,
a rock from Lillian Street,

and cemented them to all my bones,
      where they now mosaic
      my calcified infrastructure,
haunt this tiny house.

Survey on Brooms and Broomcorn

A housewife sweeps floors,
dreams arrangements
in scuffs and drags,
articulates the pause
between verse and note.

        Her body a neat broom,
whisking the floors of the Riverbank Club House,
her feet keeping continuous contact
with the scuffed boards
of the California Ball Room.

        She herself is stitched
with four rows of waxed cotton,
guitar in hand, blunt-cut hair tips
of pure broomcorn. O Rhythm Guitar
O Harmony Duet

        you delicate parlor broom:
Her heart has these contours
like beech, birch, other light wood—
turn it with gentle pressure;
Sand it and call it ordinary care.
Stain it; call it a song.

All About Birds: An Elegy

for Jamal Khashoggi

O, to send you off with towels
     and handkerchiefs waving
         in the breeze, facing the east

at sunrise. Listen to the doves vocalize;
     notice how they inflate the throat
no matter where they perch, whether statuary

     or the strained ropes: They sing. All this tug
and release, this pull and tension,
     this frayed twine—

ghosts
     have always been walking
through the spaces of our home. This is how the place

     burnt itself down:
         room by immaculate room,
            fist by bone, memory after
            derelict memory
     became words on thin paper
paste-glued to street light posts, announcing

     your grandmother's funeral,
     your uncle's funeral.
Words that made a life on the page

now lambent futile stars,

gold findings. But not *your* funeral, my dear.
                    Which galaxy

contains you now? Which bird's throat?
                    In the pines,
the wind swept through the thicket,
            and I saw.

I saw.
            I sank into breath and time,
                    even though the history of the world

is a murder ballad
                with *pinus mugo, pinus brutia,* and mourning doves
            on the gravel as witness.

                    Remember to etch images
            and locations into your mind—
this poem is a memory palace:

In the first place
            refers, my love,
to the peaches we ate on the balcony;
            refers, my love,
to the months you first loved me,

            when the doves in the jacaranda
already knew.

The Region Was Mapped from the Air

She holds a matchbook a composition book
and a transit map to the underground tunnels
of her original city its dimly lit corridors

subject to flooding to the enclosed
staircase with a landing and right turn
halfway to the top level to the threshold
where she finds the black kitten
cold to the mattress in the corner where she rests
after an abortion waiting for appetite

to return the map fails to mark the exact moment
the space shuttle explodes
the radio broadcast
the sudden awakening
the way one boy works
his way off the floor and onto her body

their change in elevation forcing dams
to overspill they are on the highest floors
so many times she ascends
Old Crow bottle in coat pocket a question
mark in the air where she drinks vodka
with record-store guys

where she is pregnant where she
falls on wet sidewalk ripping her tights I am telling you
where fallout shelters are located
where he is asked to leave the car when he says but
I want it and are you kidding me
because this is the place

where she breaks a glass every day
they slip from her outstretched hands
it seems onto the hard floor
the incidents recorded faithfully
in the notebook of broken things
and even when he tells her

you are such a
it doesn't register
as much as glass shards do
their inevitable explosions
on hard linoleum floor that place
where wavy lines mark the shifting borders
of this new country this body
the flesh that wipes entire cities
off the map

Prayer for You on the Way to Wherever You're Going

While you're on your way to wherever you are going,
make time for interesting civic slogans,
kind tones of voice from your offspring,
and tender pork chops at dinner, as you wait
for those children to grow;

and on your way, don't forget
to wave at the passing cars, the '62 Rambler Ambassadors,
the '57 Chevy Impalas—lowered or not—the '49 Chevy pickup
with the two-tone paint job and its wine press in the wood-slat bed
on which you chipped your front tooth;

meanwhile, on your way to fully dying in this city,
don't forget to stand at the side of the street
watching the veterans parade by,
the group ever-smaller year by passing year—
and to think about what that means;

and on the way to wherever your route ends, remember
the urban forestry division and its cherry-pickers taking crews up high,
clearing out the mistletoe taking hold in your soul. It roots
to your higher self, takes in your exhalations
and thrives.

And on the way to wherever you are going,
don't forget to design the official flag of your being.

Do it with your own brand of thinking, all of the
small sadnesses mixed with triumph, your flag waving
in the same air we breathe, here in this city—

And while you are on the way
to wherever you are going, bless each face you meet,
the creases at the bottom corners of both eyes; bless
the line of the lips where they meet. Curve your own mouth
into a shape, a symbol, the flag of this singular moment,

when you meet your neighbors at every corner—in the Virginia Corridor,
in Dry Creek; you are here in this moment, you fill it, are filled;
you are firmly twined around the tree trunk of time. And so,
on the way to wherever you are going, you find yourself
always arriving here, where you were, where you are.

Historic Structure Report

Addressed to the building at 833 Tenth Street, Modesto

The asparagus fern of commerce
overspills your planters,
thrives along your bones,
while inside, borrowed-money ball gowns

and loggia daydreams consider a dance. Your glass,
columns, composite floors, and floral-stamped metal—
those vertical striations raked in cement—
all expressions of a certain mid-century mindset.

Let me enter through the south door.
Usher me in with your hush and opaque starburst
truth. Accept my payments at the counter,
for I've been saving up for you. Hush, my monolith—

I took notes; I know your mystery.
I've heard your whispers,
spelunked the caverns
inside us both.

I've imagined walking up your grand staircase
and finding your soul there along the sweeping mezzanine.
Give me your hand underneath bubble light:
Let us both dazzle, fully lit at night.

Oramil's Dream

I am a founding father of this city,
which rediscovers itself every day

as new arrivals check in at the station,
and children take rations to their tents

then play under the bridge
watchful, waiting for the missionaries

to arrive with clothes and salvation,
waiting for their inheritance of sidewalk,

of median strip. I am a war deserter
reviewing your appeal for a doorway

rain gutter endowment of bedroom
window a brick fireplace bequest,

who changed my name
and never looked back,

who watches still my children huddled,
carbonsmudge eyes hardening to knives.

Even now I withhold
what always belonged to you.

The Great Plow-Up

Hold back the rushing minutes, make the wind lie still
Don't let the moonlight shine across the lonely hill
Dry all the raindrops and hold back the sun
My world has ended, my baby's gone

—Hazel Houser, "My Baby's Gone"

water wealth contentment health

H_2O

in this city of drought
or atmospheric river,

you lean against me,
slightly behind

my body, hand
in pocket.

I superimpose a smaller
form against your height.

Meanwhile, shadow
selves behind the smiles

arrange this other shape,
this fractal of us—

a sentient creature
threatening its own weather,

a willy-nilly water cycle—
inevitable torrent.

$

If my credit score were higher,
we'd be married, Modesto. You
were my first choice, the most
valuable asset in a field
of questionable possibilities.

∞

For a two-month period,
        she felt calm
inside the snow-globe
        fog world
when the clock struck
        onion-scented midnight.

"Epigenetics has transformed the way we think about genomes . . ."
Oh really, Modesto? The prefix *epi*
("over," "outside of," "around")

suggests factors layered
atop the map. Beloved city,
what a wonder! In what tender
ways do your fingers press
into our very genes
to make a point about chaos?
Each twinkle gland
comprises a point on your elevated
arch, builds an altar to Our Lady
of Activated Cells.

Your downtown
a sensitive gut-brain
signaling neurotransmitters
to destinations unknown,
keeping us out of range,
barely within love's reach
while we walk
beside monsters
and stopped trains. Still,
we endeavor,
incandescent.

Root-Cause Failure Analysis

Define *influx:*
an arrival of or entry of large numbers of people
or an inflow of water into a river, lake, or the sea—

please consider all the ways a thing can go wrong,

the way *human devastation syndrome*
can and does refer to children,

temporary emergency influx shelters
built to house human overflow,

the spaces where physics, soil, scars, fluids,

and distortions intersect in the abstract.

Even approaching the task from a multidisciplinary perspective—

rising seas and methane currents—
our animal hearts break, break, break

while great blue herons are landing on
mats of soil and plants right now in the Sacramento Slough.

I am trying to tell you, my love,
we are tule berms,
created by peat moss accumulation,
dense tangle of Delta weeds, our hearts
a weathered laydown in the sloughs.

Castle of the Mountain

The nurse remarked
on the shortage of IV saline bags this year
due to the impact of Hurricane Maria
in Puerto Rico. The fluid,
an alarming red in its bag,
drips slowly into the central line
connected to your metal button port:
from bag to blood and bone.

The art therapist kneels beside you,
selecting tubes of the good acrylic paints
from her plastic supply bins.
When we learned that the red color
of doxorubicin originated from red bacteria
in the soil around a medieval castle in Italy,
I thought *the monks did it again.* Now, here we are,
infusion pump with its quiet metronome tick,

the abrupt double-beep when the bag is flat,
emptied; this weekly ritual in the black vinyl chair
on the fourteenth floor as we look out
at hawks twisting in the air
hunting pigeons. On your canvas, you paint yourself
into the corner of a brilliant pink space—
my citadel fortress, my daughter—
hovering ruby-throated
in a liquid red universe.

A Mistaken Analogy Concerning Demeter and Persephone

Out of sparkling doxorubicin red,
out of pomegranates in the front yard,

out of tent roofs down in the park,
out of her favorite redtail hunting for prey
        and that other realm to which it returns—
a false sun dogs the real sun.
She falls into the opened earth—a trick—

unceremoniously lands in this bed.
Out of the beep of the infusion machine,

out of meds that both destroy and preserve,
out of the body's interior walls
        that shed their continuous cell harvest,

out of a nightly needle in the thigh made numb with ice,
out of the cornucopia of pain,

she bites the flesh of her lovely mouth
        into a crown of flowers.

Galvanized Gutbucket

Tell me about the heart, metal chair.

     The scarred skin.

          The fibrous pericardium,
                   that biological pocket
          encasing those four chambers.
The endless receiving and discharging,
          the loosely connected tissue that binds
          many centers.

Brittle inside chest walls:
          Immersed electrodes
          in the same bucket can surely never
                   touch.
The science of defibrillation:
          electricity's signal.

                   O toppled statue of terror,
          galvanize me, give me form—
animate flatline love, Frankenstein me.

Animal, Vegetable, Mineral

You don't dare look at the shroud
across the mediastinum

behind the breastbone.
Terror builds cell by sticky cell,

the consistency of a potato, the surgeon said,
and I wondered

did he mean raw or cooked. Fear takes root,
an entire potato establishing itself

behind the breastbone.
The site of fear: the chest

as a root cellar, a vine pushing out
from the eye of a potato,

its own uncanny thing.
The tumor has a consistency,

one of not-breathing
and of panic. My fear

a tiny node of boiled potato,
such a small thing,

a small thing that swallows the entire sun.

Memory Gardens, Livermore

We visited the cemetery
the way that people now go to parks
or the mall.

The women of the family tended plots,
replacing dead flowers with fresh. They remembered them all:
Konstantin Beratlis, cheesemaker dead in his mid-fifties,
    and our own young dead:
    Theo Pete, gone at thirty-three.
    Then my own father,
    next, the wise peripatetic George the same year.

In Memory Gardens I learned what you do
when you lose the people you love. There,

    those afternoons, in the heat of summer sun,
the pedestrian smells of juniper and cut grass
mingling during graveside church services
with the priest's ritual frankincense,

    you stand quietly, riveted in place by the impossibly
angry stare of a second cousin from Fresno
who is wearing her sharpest mourning suit and heels

You listen to your family sing *christos anesti*
    because everyone seems to die in the spring.

You mouth the words, every now and then
vocalizing a word you know in Greek,

while Memory Gardens sings Gregorian chants
in an indeterminate background soundscape

      punctuated by hot rods on East Avenue.
Each in-ground cemetery vase
hides skeleton keys and rolled pages
from a vintage barber's catalog.

      Since earliest memory,
my very-much-alive grandmother's photo
was already mounted in place
on the family headstone, prepaid years before
at the time of K's death and burial. I learned what
practical people do in times of sorrow.

      Memory Gardens has hopes for us,
wants our release from grief, wants the collapse of time,
wants us to quit stepping on the dead
with our large, impertinent feet.

How to Possibly Find Something or Someone by Praying

1.
Make an earnest effort
to look for whatever you want.
I'm a typewriter wreck on the highway;
don't look at me.
You are throwing your voice
into every corner as I hunt and peck
the light fantastic.

2.
After you are confident that you have searched carefully for what-
ever it is that is lost, then it is time to ask for help.

Sweep up all the dust, get itchy with longing for the object your
heart desires, bend like wood, get bent into hairpin side chair with
rustic legs.

Make monuments of your shiver state. Open your tender, beseeching
mouth.

You are a baby bird.

3.
People find that praying to St. Anthony works
the majority of the time. This is not a magic trick;

faith is needed. If faith cannot be found,
you should design an entire city to contain

what has been lost; construct a cathedral in its
honor. Build your set, explore

the catacombs of loss. Method–act pain
into its own book of psalms; preserve it

in the birdcage of your ribs.
Hold still for life.

Republic of Tenderness and Bread

for Modesto

Each Tuesday afternoon a loaf of bread is placed
on a pillow of towels in the ice chest
outside my front door. The rules:

> Bring a meal between 4:30 and 6
> and don't ring the bell. The sun's already

going down, the heater cycling on,
the machine hum like Mom's Singer,
whose slow motor chugs, lumbers,

> as she pedal-controls the speed,
> her foot easing into a new country.

Now my daughter and I live in a new country.
We sit on the sofa, blankets wrapped around our shoulders,
her skin a smooth alabaster goth after weeks of chemo.

> The black dog barks; we listen to sounds on the porch
> as someone approaches. Now the ice-chest lid—

hinges squeak, items stacked inside. The lid closes, gently;
a car drives off. And for a moment the thought:
This is not my daughter, not her bare head bobbing down the hallway.

> This is not her pill organizer on the kitchen counter.
> We hear the low churn—the heater cycles on,

and Michele drives from another city
with a Tupperware of vegetable soup,
delivering a balanced meal—

      a dinner with wine—Cortney brings coffee beans
      so that I never run out of the drug that keeps me afloat.

When people you know well (and some not so well)
feed you every night for months straight,
you want to embrace everyone

      for an inappropriate length of time.
      You want to reshape all these awkward relations

into a new economy of simple care,
this ancient rhythm you fall into,
with stew and coffee and bread.

The edge of the sea

is where we went to escape
bacteria and viruses,
where you rode a golf cart
through damp seaside flora—

I imagined spores and molds
drifting through ocean air
destined straight for your compromised
lungs.

By the edge of the sea
we could almost escape
as long as I could wipe down
every surface with bleach;

we could almost escape
when you ran, walked, cried,
tied a scarf around your bare head,
unfastened yourself from the heart

of that yellow chemistry
and walked into the lapping foamy waves

Regret Bench

He said that his kingdom was not of this world
So what is the profit of silver and gold
So cheap it will seem on that great judgment day
Where fire and great heat will melt it away

—Hazel Houser, "Men Are So Busy"

A Unified Theory of Everything
While Listening to *Science Friday*

Let's rebuild our cells with clay and time,
save ourselves from that imminent calamity,
watch falcons strike with steep plunge-dives

while docking ports keep us dead and surviving.
I'm wired and woven into the tapestry,
rebuilding this heart with clay and time

even though narrative's a trick of the mind.
I'm learning to die in the Anthropocene.
Let falcons fool hapless families with camouflaged dives,

now a feedback loop to hasten the crash.
Heat me by degrees and release my useless anomie.
The ground gives way; it's just clay and time.

The infusion clinic's no place to tell lies,
but yes, you're the painful sun in my galaxy—
whose velocity vector is aimed right here in the falcon's fall.

In your curtained-off space fourteen stories high,
this small despair holds the entire galaxy.
We built this shrine from clay and time.
Strap a camera to my back; watch me swoop and dive.

How many times have I driven

north on Highway 99
into the arms of this or that man

for the promise of rocks
on the shore to meet

my chaos waves
only to have the shore dissolve

to a tidal pool of sea stars
a disappearing bench

where two lovers sit
in full view of leisure boaters

like statues of lust
how many times did I drive south on Highway 99

where the valley crinkles
into reverse alluvial plain

then straight down to the Park Bar
my own reverse migration

over the poppy-washed Grapevine
my chest fully open

a wrecked guitar stand in the back
waiting for takers

Conversation with a Lover About the Louvins

You don't get it: Desire's an underground fruiting body,
this song its presentable iteration. That bodes well,
don't you think? I love you under the front porch

lattice, my Blind Blake. Don't squander it. First,
step down into street; in darkness delight. Next,
rye paired with pear, the pair pared

to leather, bluejean and thigh. Hazel's rules
for songwriting: Dip from the deeper wells. Well, we are.
Let us remember the frayed interior of her

collar, the resoled boots, the space where she
pressed through to us, grew from your spindly tomato
plant into our blind unminding. Reminder: From the banks

of the river Jordan, she's minding our constant unwinding,
creating a hall of fame of our neglect. On this Mother's Day,
my heart's on holiday with that Modesto housewife

who only now, O country gospel boy, wrote about this,
what she wrote, what it's about, what about it, until it
drains from my eye, that vision,

that seismic morning drinking coffee
from a bowl while squinting
in Jesus's light.

I love you in autumn

when the Modesto ash
flames arson. In spring,
San Joaquin snow
petals the orchards
into luminous dusk
moonscape. Almonds,
almonds with the short *a*.
Into these places,
O Lord, bring us taco wagons,
poetry, and love,
not necessarily in that order.
Bring us summertime's
savior, Delta breeze,
without which
our parch goes
murderously
unrelieved. Believe in me
in all seasons;
my body parts know how to make a map
of all the small towns in this valley.

I Am Disoriented and Looking at Maps

I am white noise.

I am the ambiguous space found right after leaving the tried-and-true
but before arriving in the next place.

I will rest here now on this hot asphalt, waiting for resolution;
that is, I am waiting for the earth to open up.
That is, I am waiting for my body to be swallowed whole.
That is, I am waiting for the sun to expand and engulf the inner
planets.

In preparation, I am already developing
my blindness.

From Somewhere Else

My sister lies on the carpeted tan floor
in the sunlit patch of sculpted beige
cut-and-loop pile playing with hand-me-down

Barbies like most girls of a certain age,
unsnapping with small fingers
their custom-made fifties clothes.

Mom's working at her sewing machine,
dropping pins into the carpet;
every now and then we are stabbed.

I sneak a stool to the hallway closet
and find the Nancy Drews
my father has stacked on the top shelf

in front of the handgun
I was not supposed to find.
I wonder why everyone except me

is a seamstress in my family,
knows how to hem, chain stitch—
our clothes threaded by that other language,

this shadow exiled otherness—
blind stitch backstitch whipstitch—

our matching clothes chalk-mark
      this permanent line.

We Write Songs in His Rent-Controlled Apartment

Always walking downstairs into below-street-level homes.
   That's where the melody takes me. But this time I walked
myself up to the second floor, over speckled granite, just to the door.
   Then the other took my hand and led me
through that doorway, to that room of tomato flowers
   that never quite set, sad stems spindly in the window.
A glimpse of pedal steel, covered in sheet. Silver tree. Alphabet. Bluesmen.
   I beseech thee, stainless quivering leg of bone and ligament,
allow me to finish the entire song. I'm no lead guitarist.
   Is the song better served by a sharp tidy solo
or the Janus tremolo of pure feeling? I wonder.
   Do not counter with what is known. Fingerpick the hell out of
those strings, in this small apartment with its brief luxuries
   and cigarette smoke. Let the song hang from the ceiling;
I might not have the air.

Anecdote of a Table

after Wallace Stevens's "Anecdote of a Jar"

She sets a table on Walnut Ave

      and square it is, in a darkened room—

her lipstick and clip assemblage reorders the spiderweb corners

      into symmetrical mosaic

while the megacell of his storm travels directly to her shantytown square.

      The downslope winds begin:

from the mountains to the plains at night, they draw into eddies

      the action figures and lovers' drawings.

Comic books in archival bags fall into chaos currents,

      and magic is a calling card for desires enacted in bullet time.

      She stays still while he dissociates, enters bodies,

becomes optical illusion.

Meanwhile, the scene on table mountain is katabatic—

      from the plains to the mountains in the morning,

tabletop tableau is the threshold,

the elevated mesa of smoke ritual and forgetting,

the stage on which characters improv sketches of despair.

One reaches into a purse

and proffers a notebook of tight grids that cannot be countenanced.

The other hyperventilates,

collapses, and later awakens, ready to reflect. The set, a simple household:

a spoon, a plastic bag, Styrofoam cups near the door.

Sundry items float through dust motes, connect in invisible webs

to the walls,

are hinges on which the action pivots.

Let her transcribe such feelings

into a pattern of squares and curved lines.

Let her form a topographic map of this blind country,

this nowhere else.

Fracture Mechanics

You can drop me
after drilling holes
in my steel beams,
cut into my brittle metal
with limited understanding
of fracture mechanics—
I needed to know this,
I needed to know.

The nature of the failing
must be understood
through the lens of
modern material science:
        your core,
        your one-mindedness,
your application of force
to enable the crack
to propagate. This was a lesson, no? I needed
to know, know this onesidedness, this lesson,
this less-than,
this appearance of.

Sudden load
weld access
weld determination
cracktip opening displacement—

weld me to you, unerringly.
Unerringly, you said. And yet.
       An abundance of caution
          was not applied.

Ode on a BIC Turntable

The sun, just a teenager then,
filtered magic through vertical blinds,
                shone its enchantment.

                In the golden hour,
I am making out in my bedroom
with our local teen misfit, my first of many—
                innocence, innocence in the golden hour.

                But it's not the stubble of chin
and pinch of braces I most recall. The records on the turntable
have my full attention: Black Market Clash,
                B. B. King, Freddie King—

                O Brent,
ruler of my young poetry heart and my sister's, too.
To the boy who walked through streets of my city
                with his guitar slung over his shoulder

                on the streets of my city,
alive in the nowhere space bridging childhood home
                and that tiny trashed cottage in the alley,

Surf Kitchen, whence you help me procure weed
in the darkness of Graceada Park where I walked
                with impractical heels,
                        dye-black hair teased high,

to Bob Marley's *Exodus* and Neil Young
and my own imminent departure from this medium-sized city.
Soon, but not soon enough:
I am teetering,
　　my stylus always sharp.

Ode to North Bay Inn

Against your sturdy walls
people have been, are, will be
in slam ceremonious,
the insistent knee

between thighs,
other objects
of human cognition.
Your interior its own

ecosystem, a matted place
where certain life
forms thrive:
the hunger of eyes

the love of throats,
backs, timeless
important ravishments
free for the lunch hour.

On mottled brown carpet,
I used a small table,
perched there,
hoped its joints

sturdy against
the *knock-knock*,
laconic while items
stutter at table,

untethered,
atomically,
emotionally
undecided.

Instant Message with Broken Glass

We've grown hard against the years,
you and I, and now it seems I've found
you, someone who loves me without knowing me,

who sees the isolation in the hard lines bracketing my mouth,
my security hasp. Insinuate yourself, then run
up to the gate and I'll unlatch it freely

because tonight my heart is busting from loneliness
and the thought of your infusion
in a fluorescent room with nondescript others

that turns out to be a place of invention
where you experiment with the world's credulity
and answer questions with such guile and ease

it's impressive. Jesus, those wet hatchlings
nesting high in the vines start and flutter
their pathetic new wings every time someone yells

and a drunk man walks by, clearly lurching—
does he intend this or not?
Your story clicks, then falls away like the loose skin

on your cheekbones. Even as we type out the other's fears,
even as I start to put two and two together,
some things are already breaking.

Walking in the Park, We Are Beset by Insects

The dragonflies soar in
distinct planes, zippy jewels in fine
      slices of air, gliding the stratum
          just above the grass,
patrolling the universe of my knees

with organization and hover
logic. Slender spreadwing,
      powdered dancer, familiar
         bluet: It's dragonfly business
here. Each double-barreled form

waits for the sun to rise,
pumps up her morning wings and
      skims patiently, feasting
         on midges and flies. Flight
lines radiate out from our vertical selves

as we hover
and beat our wings
inside the algebra of insects,
creating our own clumsy arcs
and perfect disturbance.

A Dream About Steinhart Aquarium

On a windy day with allergens,
wind-whipped branches,
invoices and blood tests,
he recalls a night inside
that black emerald grotto, that dome of
aquarium. In possession of his
full godly powers then, he sat with her on
the black bench, their bodies oscillating
in salt and honey waves, the thick
glass concealing them from aquatic life.
Between the water's surface and the ocean's
floor, he may have engraved her skin
with a light finger trace, and she may have
scraped bitten nails across the grain
of his pants with a smile and a bending forward
as royal visitors sauntered in and out of the room,
the sunfish and occasional small shark
flitting past in dread and hunger.
The background murmur of voices plays for minutes
then the silence as she fills his hands entirely.
The mouth waters; the tide goes out.
The natural world constantly brings to the
surface its own signals and mysteries, he thinks,
even at this late hour when most of the gods
have frozen into bas-relief.

For the Jacket Left Behind

Words read in the church
hang in air like stained glass:
His mind is windows.

I hold out both sleeves,
imagine the arms inside them.
Who has lost the most?

Olive and army—
let the green be a beacon,
call up the autumn moon.

This Is How We Become

We built the world a wire framework
        of copper, knots, and wisteria. Folding and
        resistance, twisted exigencies—

Our vines burst flowers, shiver and sound—
        we are attached to our sadness,
        we are attached to our joys.

We keep a coin in the world's pocket,
examine the heads & tails, and all states of being
tossed about.

By degrees, degrees of being. Not by either/
        or, looking past the binary world. Not with one voice
        but with multiplicity.

This is how we become: I am typography,
I am proportional, not monospaced. I am the text block
and the margin,
the waves and the rocks,
the barnacles in the crags.

This is how we become: We are
        100 percent sure of our visions, know they
        reflect the shattered surface of the world.

We are 100 percent sure of our visions,
        know they will make it whole
        by holding space for possibility:

We mix, we mingle; we put everything in our measuring cup.
    We recombine
    We mutate
    We strengthen
    We boil.

This is how we become:
    We spill over/the page, our cells are used for ink.
We increase, we multiply.
We write shadows and light,
pen marks, narrative, inkstains, revolution.

This is how we become: We evolve,
    we drag you in the future,
    we are a riot, a frame of skin, bone, and muscle.

We are here, intertwined, history, the present—
We are doing everything
to carry you across, to finish this page:

I am just one person.
I am holding a sign.
I am holding a pen.
I am carrying you.
I am strumming this guitar.

Dancing in Deep Time

Some songs always call: Whether
the lost pentatonic scales of *assouf,*
echoed in ghost-picked Mali blues,

or the Crows Landing dance hall *corrido*
tuba, I feel the desert blues.
Each data point I collect,

interpret, and weave into the melody
is the strand that connects me to you.
Grasslands, desert, riparian zone—

I feel the threads pull on all my selves,
each strand subject to the force
of mycorrhizal web,

that hypersensitive connector
that knows exactly what it's up to
or down for: that intimate, biological thrust

pushing us into caves of longing
in search of that one stitch, that secret knot
that binds, frays, releases. The world is not waiting

to be catalogued by scientists and librarians:
Glaciers calve, species silently cease to be. Woe be unto us:
We thought dancing did not matter.

ACKNOWLEDGMENTS

I'm grateful to Skip Heller, Doug Houser, Gerrie Bell, George Scarlett, Sara Coito, Frank M. Young, Jim Damron, Dennis Yudt, Bonnie Ohara, James McAndrews, and Jeremy Center for conversations about music, space, and science fiction, and the apocalypse for their inspiration and support. Thank you to members of Sixteen Rivers Press for their feedback on individual poems and the manuscript as a whole, and particularly to Gillian Wegener, whose counsel and enduring friendship and support have sustained me more than I can say.

California Fire & Water: A Climate Crisis Anthology (Story Street Press, 2020): "Root-Cause Failure Analysis"
Collisions VI: "wealth water contentment health"
From Whispers to Roars: "Galvanized Gutbucket"
Touchstones: Life and Times of Modesto (Community Heritage Series, 2017): "Prayer for You on the Way to Wherever You're Going"

NOTES

Almond dust: Endemic to the Central Valley almond-growing region every fall, almond dust is caused by machines that shake the trees and stir up the ground around them in order to harvest the almonds.

Assouf, also known as guitare, al gitara, teshumara, desert blues, and Tuareg rock: A distinct style of music expressing the sense of loneliness and exile of the Tuareg people following post-colonial social upheaval in the southern Sahara.

BIC turntable: British Industries Corporation introduced the first belt-drive record turntables.

Blue 59: A pseudonym and persona adopted by my dear friend Paul Christopher Riley (RIP).

Comstock: Nevada's Comstock Lode, a body of silver ore discovered in 1859, caused a silver rush to the area near Virginia City.

Corrido: A popular ballad form of song, often about socially relevant topics such as oppression, history, and the daily life of criminals. An important part of Mexican and Mexican-American culture, it is still popular today.

Deep time: A term for geologic time; introduced by John McPhee in his book *Basin and Range.*

Dust Bowl Venus is a phrase I first heard in a February 2020 presentation on world-building in science and science fiction by Katherine Buse, a PhD candidate in English and Science and Technology Studies at UC Davis. When I heard it, I knew it had to be the title of my next collection of poems about the Central Valley and its often alien nature. "Venus" is a reference to the planet, but it also alludes to the central muse of this collection, songwriter Hazel Houser.

Grapevine: A community in Kern County, California; also a steep grade on Interstate 5 known as the Grapevine. This part of I-5 connects the Central Valley with Southern California.

Hazel Houser: A songwriter and musician who came to Modesto from Oklahoma with her family during the Depression. Many of her gospel and country music songs were first recorded by the Louvin Brothers in the late fifties and subsequently by hundreds of other artists.

Hells Bells Concerto No. 1: An imaginary piece of music that takes its title from an AC/DC song.

The Louvins: The Louvin Brothers, an American musical duo composed of brothers Ira and Charlie Louvin. They are known for their fire-and-brimstone country gospel songs.

Massey Ferguson: A manufacturer of agricultural vehicles; the term is used here as a shorthand for a kind of tractor, the MF35, which first rolled out of the factory in 1957.

Modesto ash *(Fraxinus velutina* 'Modesto'*)*: A fast-growing culti-var of the Arizona ash tree, known for its shade-producing canopy and brilliant yellow leaves in the fall. Planted extensively within the city of Modesto as street trees, they are susceptible to mistle-toe, and most of them have now surpassed their fifty-to-sixty-year life span and are diseased or dying. Limbs frequently fall from the trees onto the yards, driveways, and rooftops of Modesto.

Oramil: Shorthand for the McHenry brothers, considered founding fathers of Modesto thanks to their business ventures here. After arriving in Modesto around 1850, Robert McHenry joined forces with his brother, Leonard Oramil Brewster, who had been living in Stockton.

Paganini: Niccolò Paganini (1782–1840), an Italian violinist and composer.

Pinus brutia (or Turkish pine): A conifer native to the eastern Mediterranean region.

Pinus mugo, also known as mugo pine, mountain pine, or scrub mountain pine: A conifer native to Central and southeast Europe.

Seasonal lake bed: Also known as a dry lake and created when water from other sources flows into a dry depression in the landscape; it may contain shallow water in the rainy season.

Tule berm: A shelf of tule reeds, a native plant that once blanketed the California Delta, anchored by peat moss accumulation.

Vernal pool: A small, shallow, ephemeral body of water with no permanent inlet or outlet. A unique type of wetland habitat found in some parts of the California Central Valley.

Sixteen Rivers Press is a shared-work, nonprofit poetry collective
dedicated to providing an alternative publishing avenue for
San Francisco Bay Area poets. Founded in 1999 by seven writers,
the press is named for the sixteen rivers
that flow into San Francisco Bay.

SAN JOAQUIN • FRESNO • CHOWCHILLA • MERCED • TUOLUMNE
STANISLAUS • CALAVERAS • BEAR • MOKELUMNE • COSUMNES • AMERICAN
YUBA • FEATHER • SACRAMENTO • NAPA • PETALUMA